Water for Life

Bernard Smith

Level 2

Series Editors: Andy Hopkins and Jocelyn Potter

Pearson Education Limited

Edinburgh Gate, Harlow,
Essex CM20 2JE, England
and Associated Companies throughout the world.

Pack ISBN: 978-1-4058-8444-0
Book ISBN: 978-1-4058-6791-7
CD-ROM ISBN: 978-1-4058-6790-0

This edition first published by Pearson Education Ltd 2008

1 3 5 7 9 10 8 6 4 2

Text copyright © Bernard Smith 2008

Illustrations by alademosca il·lustració / Illustration on page 9 by Jesús Alonso Iglesias

The author has asserted his moral right in accordance with the
Copyright Designs and Patents Act 1988

Set in 11/13pt A. Garamond

Printed in China
SWTC/01

Produced for the Publishers by AC Estudio Editorial S.L.

Published by Pearson Education Ltd in association with Penguin Books Ltd,
both companies being subsidiaries of Pearson Plc

Notes

2: Data from Millennium Ecosystem Assessment

11: Jones, Lewis. *Water*. Longman Structural Reader series, Longman Group 1979.

36: Abramovitz, Janet. 'Imperiled Waters, Impoverished Future: The Decline of Freshwater Ecosystems'.
Worldwatch Paper No. 128. Worldwatch Institute, March 1996.

Acknowledgements

We are grateful to the following for permission to reproduce photographs:

(Key: b-bottom; c-centre; l-left; r-right; t-top)

Alamy Images: Rachael Bowes 35; Richard Emmons 15; Panorama Media (Beijing) Ltd 26;
B&C Alexander/Arcticphoto.com: 25, 42/4, 44; **Corbis**: Atlantide Photogravel 23b; Patrick Barta 37;
Ruggero Vanni 23t; Yann Arthus-Bertrand 31; **Greenpeace UK**: John Novis 41;
Robert Harding World Imagery: Cubo Images 13cr, 13r; David Hughes 13l; National Geographic 1bc;
iStockphoto: 1bl, 1tl, 1tr, 13cl, 28; **Nature Picture Library**: Tom Mangelsen 3;
PA Photos: Associated Press 2; PA WIRE 1tc; **Panos Pictures**: Jim Holmes 40t; Gerd Ludwig 36;
Qilai Shen 1br; **Courtesy of Petro-Canada**: 30t; **Science Photo Library Ltd**: Josh Sher 10b; Tom Van Sant/
Geosphere Project/Santa Monica 8; **STILL Pictures The Whole Earth Photo Library**: Julio Etchart 17;
Ron Giling 40b; Shehzad Noorani 5; Jorgen Schytte 20; **TopFoto**: 2000 Credit 29

All other images © Pearson Education Ltd

Picture Research by Kay Altwegg

Every effort has been made to trace the copyright holders and we apologise in advance for any
unintentional omissions. We would be pleased to insert the appropriate
acknowledgement in any subsequent edition of this publication.

For a complete list of the titles available in the Penguin Active Reading series please write to your local
Pearson Longman office or to: Penguin Readers Marketing Department, Pearson Education,
Edinburgh Gate, Harlow, Essex CM20 2JE, England.

Contents

1.1 What's the book about?

1 Discuss these questions.

   a You drink and cook with water every day. Where does it come from?
   b Why is water important for life?

2 Look at these pictures and the words below them.

   a What are these words in your language?

drought

flood

ice, iceberg

hurricane, typhoon

waves

pollute, pollution

   b Talk about two of the pictures. How are these dangerous to people?

3 What other 'water words' do you know?

1.2 What's first?

The first chapter is about 'Problems with Water'. How many problems can you think of before you read? Write notes in your notebook.

CHAPTER 1

Problems with Water

*Some people say that there will be big problems in
the future. Countries will fight about water.*

Water. We drink it. We cook with it. We wash with it. We can't live
without it. It gives life to everything – to people, animals and
plants. It is everywhere: in the seas, in the rivers, in the **air** and in our
food. Most of us don't think about it very much. Water is there for us, in
our kitchens and in our bathrooms, every day.

But it is not there for everybody, and our world is changing fast. We
have to think very carefully about water, and about our use of it.

● The world's weather

So what is happening? Cars, planes, **factories** and city life are making the
world warmer every year. The air is warmer; our seas are warmer. This is
causing changes to the weather round the world. Some cold countries
are getting warmer. Some hot countries are getting hotter. Rainfall is
changing everywhere.

● Hurricanes and floods

In many countries, the warm air brings more rain and causes floods every
year. Warmer air above warmer seas takes more water up into the air.
This can cause hurricanes and typhoons. They begin over the seas and
move quickly. When they get to **land**, they can be very big. Strong winds
and heavy rainfall hit cities. They often cause big waves at sea too. When
these waves hit the land, there are bad floods. People die.

---

plant /plɑːnt/ (n/v) Trees and flowers are *plants*. You plant a tree when you put it in the
ground.
air /eə/ (n) Birds fly in the *air*. We can't live without it.
factory /ˈfæktəri/ (n) A *factory* is a big building. People make things in it.
cause /kɔːz/ (v/n) When you *cause* something, it happens.
land /lænd/ (n) We have to swim in the sea, but we can walk on *land*.

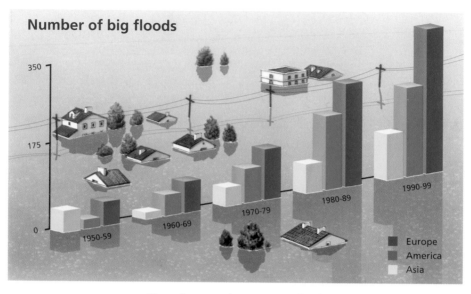

Number of big floods

350

175

0

1950-59
1960-69
1970-79
1980-89
1990-99

- Europe
- America
- Asia

Year after year, there are more floods.

In August 2005, Hurricane Katrina hit New Orleans in the United States and flooded 80% of the city. In some places the water was 6 metres high. More than 1,800 people died.

Every year, more of Bangladesh is under water in the summer. In

Hurricane Katrina floods New Orleans.

1988, more than 3,000 people died in big floods, and 3,000,000 people lost their homes. In 1991, nearly 140,000 people died when 4.5 metre waves hit the land. Some places are now under water all the time, and a lot of people die from **diseases**. This flood water is dirty, of course, and it goes into the ground water. There is water everywhere, but the Bangladeshis can't drink it.

disease /dɪˈziːz/ (n) A *disease* makes you ill. It can also kill you.

2

Not enough rain

In other countries, the problem is not *too much* rain but *not **enough***. There isn't as much rain as before, and there are long droughts. Fires start easily because trees are very dry. The fires quickly get bigger and more dangerous.

We can see these changes now. Australia has a drought nearly every year. The big rivers in the south-west are often dry. Dangerous fires start every summer near the cities of Sydney and Melbourne in the south-east, and the air in the cities is black with smoke. In the south of France and Spain too, there are droughts most summers, and there are often big fires.

Problems of ice and snow

At the same time, the ice in the north and south of the world is **melting**, so seas everywhere are slowly getting higher. The ice is melting fast. In 1980, Arctic ice was about 5 metres thick. Now it is only about 3 metres in some places. The people of the Arctic countries are losing their food and their homes. In many places the ice is too dangerous – they can't walk on it. Animals and birds are also losing their food. Many of them are dying.

Arctic animals are dying because they can't catch food.

enough /ɪˈnʌf/ (pron/det) When you don't want more of something, you have *enough*.
melt /melt/ (v) Ice *melts* into water when it gets warm.

3

In the mountains of the world, it is the same story. High mountains have snow and ice on them all year. The ice moves slowly down the mountains and melts into rivers. But the ice is melting higher up the mountains because the **Earth** is getting slowly warmer. In the mountains of Switzerland, France and Italy, there is usually snow in December for winter sports. But the snow is arriving later every year. It only stays on the highest mountains now.

● Higher seas

In 2000, the world's seas were about 30cm higher than in 1900. Some people say that in a hundred years from now the seas will be a metre higher. The ice in the Arctic and Antarctic is melting faster every year. Some people think that without the ice on Greenland, the seas will one day be seven metres higher.

How will that change our world? Countries will get smaller. When the sea is a metre higher, cities near the sea will be under water. Venice and most of London, Shanghai and New York will go. Much of the Netherlands and the Maldives will go too; about 80% of the land in the Maldives is only a metre above the sea. Bangladesh will lose 15% of its land, and 13,000,000 people will have to move. In Japan, 2,340 square kilometres of land will be under water and 4,000,000 people will lose their homes.

● Weather and food

Weather changes cause problems for **farm**ers. We **need** food, and our food comes from farms. Plants and animals on those farms need water, of course – a lot of water. When there is a drought, plants and animals die. Then people have no food. When there are floods, they can also kill plants and animals. Again, people have no food – and they can't drink the dirty ground water.

Earth /ɜːθ/ (n) The *Earth* is the name of our world.
farm /fɑːm/ (n) Fruit, vegetables and meat come from *farms*.
need /niːd/ (v) When you have to have something, you *need* it.

Our future

When floods and droughts happen only from time to time, people can usually live to the next year. They can get help from other, richer countries. But when there are floods every year, there is no answer. People have to move or die. Some people say that there will be big problems in the future. Countries will fight about water.

We know that the world is getting warmer. We know that our weather is changing. We have to do something before it is too late.

Dirty water

But the weather isn't the cause of all problems with clean water. Many people in the world don't have water in their homes. They have to walk for hours to the nearest **well** or river – and this water isn't always clean. About 80% of all the world's diseases come from dirty water. 10,000,000 people die each year from these diseases.

A long walk home with water

Every day, there are about 220,000 more people in the world, and they all need clean water. But about 600,000,000 people don't have enough water. For these people, water really is life. In a hundred years, our children's children will, perhaps, live in a very different world.

well /wel/ (n) You can take water from a *well*, under the ground.

2.1 Were you right?

1 Look at your notes for Activity 1.2 on page iv. Which problems did you *not* think of?

2 Finish these sentences with the words in the box below.

a The weather everywhere is ....

b Dirty water gives people ....

c The ice everywhere in the world is ....

d The seas are getting ....

e Big waves cause bad ....

f The number of people in the world is getting ....
every year.

floods diseases melting bigger
higher changing

2.2 What more did you learn?

Are these sentences right (✓) or wrong (✗)?

1 Factories make the air colder.

2 Typhoons begin above warm seas.

3 Bangladesh has a lot of problems with floods.

4 Australia has floods nearly every year.

5 The ice in the Arctic is getting thicker every year.

6 In 2000 the world's seas were one metre higher than in 1900.

7 The weather is changing and this is bad for farmers.

8 Every year there are about 220,000 more people in the world.

2.3 Language in use

Look at the sentence in the box. Put the words into the sentences. Use -er or more.

> The fire quickly gets **bigger** and **more dangerous**.

1 The ice in the Arctic is getting .... *thinner* .... and
   .... *more dangerous* .... (thin, dangerous)

2 The people of Bangladesh are .... every year
   because the floods are .... (afraid, high)

3 Water is .... than food. (important)

4 We have to be .... with our clean water. (careful)

5 The winters are getting .... and the summers are
   getting .... (short, hot)

6 The ice is melting quickly because the weather is ....
   (warm)

7 Every year the number of people in the world gets ....
   and the problems get .... (big, difficult)

8 Farms and factories are making some rivers ....
   every year. (dirty)

2.4 What's next?

1 Talk about the picture on page 8. What can you see? What is dark blue?
   What is white? What is green or brown?

2 Are these sentences right (✓) or wrong (✗)? What do you think?

   a Nearly all the water on our world is in the seas.

   b We can drink the water in the seas.

   c There is a lot of water in our food.

   d Animals and plants can't live without water.

   e People can live for a month without food but with water.

CHAPTER 2

A World of Water

Today, about 10% of the world's people don't have enough water. In 2025, some people say, it will be 35%.

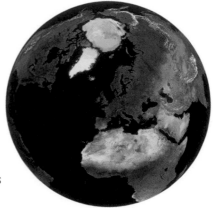

Our Earth, blue and beautiful.

Look at our Earth, the third world from the sun. It is a beautiful blue, with white in the north and the south. Here and there, there are browns and greens. But most of it is blue, because about three quarters of it is water – great seas of water. The Pacific has more than half of the world's water in it. 'Water' is perhaps a better name for our world than 'Earth'.

The large white places are ice – the Arctic in the north and the Antarctic in the south. When you stand on the ice in the Antarctic, in some places there are four kilometres of ice below your feet. 90% of the world's ice is in the Antarctic. In the Arctic it is different. The ice is a great, thin, flat plate, and it **float**s on the sea. But Greenland is a large country in the Arctic and the ice on it is two kilometres thick. There is also ice on high mountains everywhere.

This ice is **fresh** water, but the world's seas are **salt**y. This is important because we, the people on Earth, can't live without fresh water. We can't drink water from the seas.

● **Where is the fresh water?**

So what is the problem? There is a lot of water on the Earth. There are rivers. There are big **lake**s. There is rain.

float /fləʊt/ (v) Something *floats* when it stays on top of the water.
fresh /freʃ/ (adj) People and animals can only drink *fresh* water.
salt /sɔːlt/ (n) We put *salt* on our food. Salty food has a lot of salt in it.
lake /leɪk/ (n) A *lake* is a small sea of water.

But think about it. Let's put the world's water into a hundred very big glasses. Ninety-seven of those glasses have salt water from the seas in them. That leaves us only three glasses of fresh water. But two of these three glasses are the ice in the north and the south. And that leaves only one glass. More than half of the water in that glass is somewhere under the ground, and a lot of the other water is too dirty. We can drink only about 0.05% of the Earth's water.

Only half of one glass is fresh water.

More people, more problems

This doesn't change – there is no 'new' water. But every year there are about 80,000,000 more people on our Earth and they all need clean, fresh water. Today, about 10% of the world's people don't have enough water. In 2025, some people say, it will be 35%.

The biggest problems now are in Africa and the Middle East. But India, Pakistan and China have very large numbers of people and these countries are trying to make plans for the future. We don't need water only for people in their homes, of course. Farms and factories use a lot of water – more than homes. But people need food *and* work.

The use of water in the world goes up each year by about 3%, but the number of people in the world goes up by between 1% and 2%. Some countries are using 4%–8% more water every year. This will have to stop. Pollution is another big problem. Cities, farms and factories are all polluting the fresh water in rivers and lakes, so people can't drink it.

One of the first land animals

● The beginnings of life

But why do we have to have water? All life on this Earth came out of the seas. Life began in the water. First, there were very small plants and animals. Then, there were plants on the land. About 300,000,000 years later, the first small animals came out of the sea. They used the plants for food.

In time, there were more and more animals on the land, and they got bigger and bigger. Today, all people, plants and animals need water, and they carry it inside them. People are more than 60% water and some plants are 95% water. We can't live without it. Trees, flowers, animals, birds and people – all die without water.

We live the first nine months of our lives in water, inside our mothers. When we are born, we come into the air. But we carry about 40 litres of water with us all the time, inside us. Without it, we die quite quickly. Every day we lose about 2½ litres. When the weather is hot, we lose more water, and faster. And we have to put it back. Only about half of this water comes from drinking. The other half comes from our food.

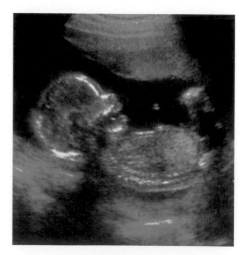

We live the first nine months of our lives in water, inside our mothers.

● Water from food

There is a lot of water in food. When you eat a chicken, three quarters of the meat is water. Many fruits and vegetables, and eggs, are nearly all water. When we cook our food in water, that gives us more.

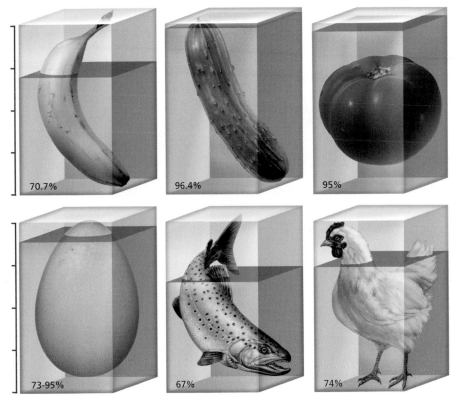

Water in our food

Doctors say that we can live for about three months without food. But we can only live for about a week without food and water. When we are working hard in hot, dry weather, we can die in hours. We die after we lose a quarter of the water inside us.

But our water has to be fresh and clean before we can drink it. Salt water will make us very ill. Dirty water can give us diseases. We need about 2½ litres of clean, fresh water every day.

3.1 Were you right?

1 Look back at Activity 2.4. Four sentences are right. Which sentence is wrong?

2 Put the words in the box into the sentences below.

ice   fresh   salty   food

a The water in the seas is ....

b Only 3% of the world's water is ....

c 2% of the world's clean water is ....

d People get a lot of their water from ....

3.2 What more did you learn?

Circle the right answers.

1 ... of the Earth is land.

   a 50%   b 25%

2 ... of the world's ice is in the Antarctic.

   a 70%   b 90%

3 ... of the people on Earth today don't have enough water.

   a 10%   b 25%

4 The number of people on the Earth goes up each year by about ... .

   a 2%   b 5%

5 There are about ... litres of water inside every person.

   a 40   b 20

6 A chicken is about ... water and a fish is about ... .

   a 60%   b 75%   c 65%   d 80%

3.3 Language in use

Look at the sentence in the box. Finish each sentence below with the best words. Write the letters, a–f.

> This ice is fresh water, **but** the world's seas are salty.

1 There is a lot of fresh water on our Earth, …

2 We can live for months without food, …

3 The ice on the Arctic seas is thin, …

4 There are a lot of lakes and rivers, …

5 Many plants and animals live on the land all the time, …

6 There is a lot of water on our Earth, …

    a but 97% of it is in the seas.
    b but we can only live for days without water.
    c but cities, farms and factories are polluting them.
    d but they need water for life.
    e but on Greenland it is very thick.
    f but more than half of it is under the ground.

3.4 What's next?

The next chapter is about fresh water. Where do we get it from?

1 Write the words for these under the pictures.

……………………… ……………………… ……………………… ………………………

2 Discuss other ideas.

CHAPTER 3

Fresh Water from Rain

There is thirty times more water in ground water than in the world's rivers and lakes.

Everybody has to have clean water. So where does it come from? It comes, of course, from rain.

But there are always problems with rain. In some places it doesn't rain for months; in other places – or in the same places – it suddenly rains for days. In countries across the centre of Africa and in south Asia, heavy rain usually starts to fall in the middle of June. It rains every day for two or three months and there are floods. But farmers can then use the land. In the other months of the year there is not much rain. It is very hot and dry and there is not enough water. In some places in north Africa and the west of Australia, it doesn't rain for years.

For every person in Europe and the United States, 3,000 to 6,000 litres of rain falls every day. But it doesn't always fall in the right places. A lot of it falls in mountains, and most people don't live in the mountains. The rain water runs into the ground or into rivers, and the rivers take it away to the sea. We also lose a lot of rain because it falls in the sea.

● Why does it rain?

There is always water in the air. When you put wet clothes out in warm air, they get dry. After it rains on the roads, a lot of the water goes up into the air. You can see it.

This happens because the sun is taking the water from the ground into the air. The air takes up water from the seas too, and this water is fresh, not salty. The salt stays in the sea. Warm air can carry more water than cold air. When the air gets colder, it starts to lose the water. Then we see **cloud**s.

---

cloud /klaʊd/ (n) You can see *clouds* in the sky. Sometimes rain falls from them.

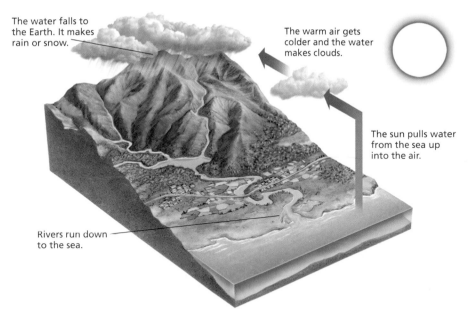

The water falls to the Earth. It makes rain or snow.

The warm air gets colder and the water makes clouds.

The sun pulls water from the sea up into the air.

Rivers run down to the sea.

Water from the sea makes rain and this runs back to the sea.

The air moves in the wind. Then, when warm air meets high ground, it goes higher. The warm air gets colder and the water in the air makes clouds. The clouds get colder and darker, and the water gets heavier. Then it starts to rain. When the air is very cold, it snows. Rain or snow falls to the ground and a lot of it runs into rivers. The rivers run into the sea. Then it all starts again.

● Water in the air

It doesn't have to rain. When wet air meets something cold, water falls on it. Look at your car in the early morning, or the trees in your garden. After a cold night, everything is wet with fresh water from the air. This is clean water. In countries without much rain, they often drink this water.

Water from the air on a cold morning

15

In Tunisia the weather is very dry, but in the early mornings the ground is often wet. In some places people can plant fruit trees and the trees do well.

● Rain water – clean or dirty?

But is rain really clean water? Can we drink it? The answer is usually, yes. But think about the rain after it falls. Water in rivers and lakes is fresh, but it isn't always clean. Dirty water runs into them from cities, factories and farms. So we have to clean the water before we can drink it.

Sometimes the air moves through smoke and dirty air above factories. Then the water in it gets dirty too. Later, when it falls, the rain can kill trees on the land and fish in lakes.

● Water from the ground

A lot of rain runs into the ground, not into rivers, and it stays there. When we find this ground water, we can **pump** it up. Usually, it is clean and fresh. More than half of the water in European and North American homes and workplaces comes from ground water.

Lake

Ground water

Ground water is usually clean

pump /pʌmp/ (v/n) You can *pump* water from one place to another place.

Drivers take water from pumps to villages.

Sometimes the water is only two or three metres under the ground; sometimes it is a long way down.

In the hottest and driest countries of the world, ground water is very important. In the countries of north Africa there is very little rain, but under the ground there are great lakes of fresh water. For hundreds of years, north Africa had rain, and the rain stayed under the ground. There were rivers, trees and a lot of people. Today, the people of north Africa pump this water up and use it.

Saudi Arabia and other dry countries also use ground water. Drivers take it from the pumps to the small villages.

● Water from wells

There is thirty times more water in ground water than in the world's rivers and lakes. People pump up ground water from old and new wells. Every year in the United States, there are 500,000 new wells.

But ground water will not always be there. When it rains, some water goes back into the ground. But this happens slowly. Sometimes there is no water in the wells. The wells are dry. There are other problems too. Near the sea, salt water can run into the ground water. Then the wells are salty.

More and more people need more and more water. One day, there will perhaps be no ground water in some countries, or it will be too dirty for them.

4.1 Were you right?

Look back at Activity 3.4. Which of these are not in the pictures? Circle them.

| a lake | a well | ice | snow | rain | a river | water in the air |

4.2 What more did you learn?

1 Circle the right words in these sentences.

a Warm air *loses / carries* more water than cold air.

b Rain falls when the warm air goes across a *mountain / lake*.

c Wet air leaves fresh water on *cold / warm* things.

d Rain water is *always / sometimes* clean.

e The ground water under the Sahara is very *old / dirty*.

f Ground water *will / will not* always be there for us.

g Wells near a *lake / sea* are sometimes salty.

2 Draw lines from the words to the right places in the picture.

| the sun | the sea | a river | rain | clouds |

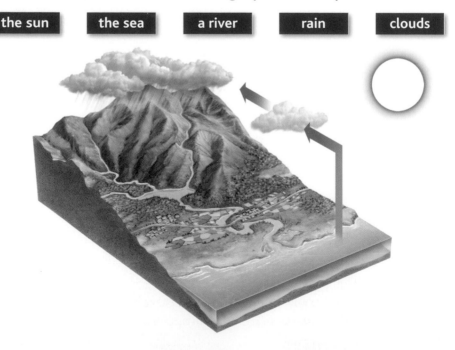

4.3 Language in use

Look at the sentences in the box. Put the word on the right in the right place in each sentence.

> There is **always** water in the air.
> They **often** drink this water.

1 People don't ª....*usually*.... live ᵇ........................
  in the mountains.

  | usually |

2 Rain ª........................ is ᵇ........................
  clean water.

  | usually |

3 The water in the air ª........................ goes
  ᵇ........................ through smoke.

  | sometimes |

4 In the early morning, the ground ª........................
  is ᵇ........................ wet.

  | often |

5 Ground water ª........................ is ᵇ........................
  only three or four metres under the ground.

  | sometimes |

6 Ground water will ª........................ not
  ᵇ........................ be there.

  | always |

7 There are ª........................ problems ᵇ........................
  with pollution.

  | often |

4.4 What's next?

The next chapter is about lessons from the past. In the past, these people moved water by waterways. Which people did this first? Number them, 1–4.

Persians   Romans   Europeans   Egyptians

19

CHAPTER 4

Lessons from the Past

When there were more people on Earth, some moved away
from the rivers. They learned about ground water.

For thousands of years, people made their homes next to rivers. They had to have fresh water for people, plants and animals. When rain didn't fall, a river always gave them water. The first people with towns and farms lived in Mesopotamia (now Iraq), between the Tigris and the Euphrates rivers.

The people of Egypt lived next to the River Nile because the river water made farming easy. Every year, after the rains in the mountains of Africa, the Nile flooded the land next to the river and made it good for farming. Farmers cut small waterways from the river across their land. These carried water to the plants. Sometimes farmers made pumps. These pumped water out of the river and on to the farmland. They were small pumps and a man could work them. Later, there were bigger pumps and an animal worked them.

When there were more people on Earth, some moved away from the rivers. They learned about ground water. They made wells and took fresh water from them for their animals and plants. In many countries people take their water from these same old wells today. They have to carry it to their homes on their heads or on the backs of animals. Often they have to carry it for kilometres.

An old well in Niger

● The first waterways

In about 2500 BC*, the people in Persia (now Iran) needed water for their farms. There was not much rain there. There were no rivers near their homes and farms, and the ground water and the wells were a long way away, near the mountains. So they moved the water from the mountains to their villages.

First they went to the high ground and studied it carefully. They looked for wet ground or green plants – for a possible place for a well. When they found water, they made more wells, dry wells, every 30 to 50 metres away from the first well. They called the first well the 'mother well'.

Then they made a way through the ground between the bottoms of the other wells. The wells got shorter and shorter and in the end they came out above the ground. Then the Persians carefully broke through to the bottom of the mother well. This was dangerous because the mother

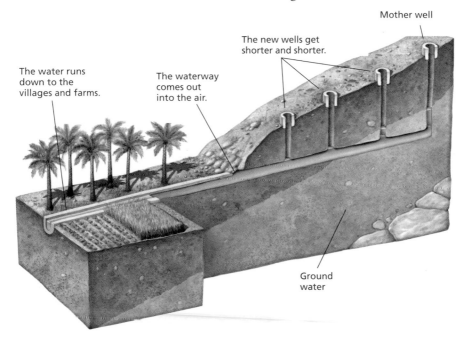

Mother well

The new wells get shorter and shorter.

The water runs down to the villages and farms.

The waterway comes out into the air.

Ground water

The falaj *or* qanat *carries ground water to the villages and farms.*

* BC: years before Christ was born

21

well had water in it. But when they broke through, the water ran from well to well and out onto the land below. Then the Persians built a waterway across the land and carried the water to their villages and farms. Some of these waterways were a hundred kilometres long.

These people didn't stay in Persia. They took their clever ideas to Arabia and built waterways there too. Three thousand years later, a lot of these waterways are working in Iran and Arabian countries. In Iran they call them *qanats*. There are thousands of kilometres of them there and three quarters of Iran's fresh water comes from them. In Arabia they call them *falajes*.

Falajes *bring life to the land near them.*

In Oman, there are about 4,000 of these *falajes*. They are 2,500 years old, and working today. Some of them run for 10 kilometres under the ground from the mother well. Then the clean, fresh water from the mountains runs for 20 or 30 kilometres through farms and villages.

Five hundred years later, the Romans also used waterways, but in a bigger and better way. They brought fresh water from the Appenine Mountains to their cities. At one time there were nine waterways into

The Aqua Claudia, near Rome, in Italy

the city of Rome. One of them, the Aqua Claudia, was 72 kilometres long, and for 15 kilometres it went over great bridges.

The Romans took these ideas from Italy into other European countries. There are great Roman waterways today in France and Spain. The Pont du Gard brought water more than 50 kilometres to the city of Nîmes, in France. It is the highest Roman waterway in Europe. It has three bridges and is 49 metres high.

All cities have to have fresh water, and the water has to come from somewhere. Usually it comes from rivers, lakes and ground water. It runs into the cities through big waterways under the ground. Today, there are great waterways in nearly every country in the world. They carry water, usually under the ground, to the people in every town and city.

The Pont du Gard, the highest Roman waterway in Europe

5.1 Were you right?

Look back at Activity 4.4, and then at these answers:

Put the right words into these sentences.

a The .... learned from the Romans.

b The .... built waterways with long, high bridges.

c The .... cut waterways from the River Nile.

d The .... called their waterways *qanats*.

5.2 What more did you learn?

Are these sentences right (✓) or wrong (✗)?

1 The River Nile floods every six months.

2 The people of Mesopotamia lived between two big rivers.

3 A well has ground water in it.

4 A *falaj* carries ground water from a mother well to farms
   and villages.

5 The Aqua Claudia carried water from Rome to the Appenine
   mountains.

6 The Pont du Gard is the longest Roman waterway in Europe.

5.3 Language in use

Look at the sentence in the box, and then at the questions and answers. Write the questions below.

> It has three bridges and is 49 metres high.
>
> **How many** bridges has it got? It has three bridges.
>
> **How high** is it? It is 49 metres high.

1 How .... ?

The waterway is 7 kilometres long.

2 How .... ?

Oman's *falajes* are 2,500 years old.

3 How .... ?

Three quarters of Iran's fresh water comes from *qanats*.

4 How .... ?

There are 4,000 *falajes* in Oman.

5 How .... ?

The Aqua Claudia was 72 kilometres long.

5.4 What's next?

Chapter 5 is about ice and icebergs. Discuss these questions and write your ideas below.

a Where do you find icebergs?
b Are they dangerous?
c Can we get fresh water from them?

Notes

Dams, Ice and Other Answers

*Can ships pull a large iceberg from the ice shelves in Antarctica
to Saudi Arabia? How big will it be when it gets there?*

W e can't make more water. We can, perhaps, find new ground
water. We can also stop polluting our fresh water and use it more
carefully. But are there other answers to the problem of fresh water?

● Dams

There is a lot of fresh water in rivers and lakes. In the end, this water
runs into the sea and we lose it. But we can stop it going into the sea.
The best way is a **dam** across a river; behind the dam there is a big lake of
fresh water. People are building more and more dams every year, and the
new lakes give us more fresh water.

The Wanjiazhai Dam on the Yellow River, China

● The world's ice

The use of ice is another possible answer. Our Earth is always changing.
It takes thousands of years but, very slowly, it gets colder or warmer.
When it gets very cold, we call this an 'ice age'. There is thick ice over a
lot of the Earth – not only in the Arctic and Antarctic. This ice is fresh
water, from rain and snow; there is no salt in it.

dam /dæm/ (n) A *dam* is a big wall across a river.

Between the ice ages, the Earth is very warm. There is very little ice and there are trees and green plants in the Arctic. We are living today about 10,000 years after the last small ice age. At that time, there was ice over most of the north of Europe. Now the weather is slowly getting warmer and the ice on the Earth is melting.

Do you remember our hundred glasses of water? Only three glasses had fresh water in them. The other glasses had salt water from the seas. And in two of the three glasses of fresh water was the ice in the north and south of the Earth. This ice is clean, fresh water.

In the north and south

Usually, when things get colder, they get smaller. But when water changes to ice, it gets a little bigger. So ice floats on water.

In the Arctic today, a large plate of ice floats on the sea. It gets bigger in winter and smaller in summer, but in its thickest places it is only about five metres thick. There is a lot more ice on Greenland, a large country in the Arctic.

But most of the ice on the Earth is in the south, in the Antarctic. Antarctica is land, not a sea. It is the coldest land on Earth. It has 90% of the world's ice and 70% of the world's fresh water. It is as big as the United States, and it gets bigger in the winter, with shelves of ice over the sea round it. In the summer, it gets smaller when a lot of the new ice melts.

There are mountains in Antarctica, and many are more than 2,000 metres high. The ice on them is two or three kilometres thick, and it is all fresh water. It is very old and very clean.

Icebergs

In the spring and summer, when the ice begins to melt, it moves slowly down from the mountains. It breaks, and great thick mountains of ice float away. These icebergs can sometimes be dangerous for ships. Some icebergs are really big. One was 335 kilometres long and 97 kilometres wide – bigger than Belgium!

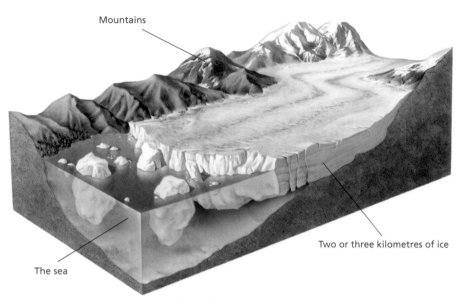

Mountains

Two or three kilometres of ice

The sea

The ice breaks into icebergs.

A lot of the ice in the south of the Earth, about a third of it, is in the great 'ice shelves' round Antarctica. These shelves also break into icebergs. Some icebergs are green or blue. But when there is a little air in the ice, they are white.

In the north, many icebergs come from Greenland. They float down into the Atlantic in the summer months. When you see an iceberg in the sea, you only see its top. Nearly all of it is below the water.

Some icebergs are very big. Air in the ice makes them white.

In April 1912, the *Titanic,* a great, new ship with 2,228 people on it, was on its way to the United States from Britain. It was the biggest ship in the world at that time. In the middle of the night it hit a big iceberg and in three hours it was at the bottom of the sea. More than 1,500 people died. Today, when ships go between Europe and the United States in the summer months, they move to the south, away from the Arctic. The journey is longer, but they don't meet icebergs.

The icebergs slowly melt in the sea, but they don't stay in one place. The winds and the seas move them, sometimes 25 kilometres in a day. The icebergs can move across the seas for many years and can go thousands of kilometres. They slowly get smaller and smaller, of course, but one iceberg from the south arrived near Rio de Janeiro, a journey of 5,500 kilometres. And an iceberg from the north made a journey of 4,000 kilometres to Bermuda.

Every year, thousands of icebergs leave the ice shelves in the Arctic and the Antarctic and float away across the seas. In every iceberg are thousands of litres of fresh, clean water.

● Fresh water from icebergs

The Titanic *hit an iceberg in the Atlantic.*

In July 1977, thirty men met in Paris. They wanted to discuss possible answers to water problems. Can ships pull a large iceberg from the ice shelves in Antarctica to Saudi Arabia? How big will it be when it gets there? Can people then use it for fresh water? This use of icebergs was not a new idea. The people of Peru did it before 1900. But the journey to Saudi Arabia is longer.

They tried it. They pulled some icebergs north to Saudi Arabia. It was difficult, slow and very expensive. After that, they stopped trying. The journey was too long and cost too much money.

But today, more than thirty years later, we really need more fresh water. In Australia there are more and more droughts. People there are discussing this question again. The icebergs of Antarctica are quite near south Australia. Perhaps the journey will not be too difficult or expensive now.

A boat pulls an iceberg. It's difficult, slow and expensive.

● Rain from clouds

What other answers are there to the problem of fresh water? In some countries, when there is a bad drought, they try to make rain. They fly aeroplanes with **chemicals** above clouds. When the chemicals fall into the clouds, they sometimes make rain. But first, you need clouds, and often there are no clouds in the sky. Also, it is expensive and does not always work.

Chemicals fall into the clouds and make rain.

chemicals /ˈkemɪkəlz/ (n pl) *Chemicals* can clean dirty water or make plants bigger and stronger.

Fresh water from the sea

You can, of course, take the salt out of sea water. This is not a new idea; it is more than fifty years old. It needs a large factory. Salt water from the sea goes in and fresh water comes out. The salt goes back into the sea. There are about 7,500 of these factories in the world today and people are building more in many countries. There are a lot of them in north African countries, but 60% are in the Middle East – a quarter of them in Saudi Arabia. Saudi Arabia has the biggest factory; it can make 580,000,000 litres of fresh water every day. 70% of the country's fresh water comes from these factories.

Australia has plans for a big, new factory too. It will make 500,000,000 litres of fresh water a day. It is expensive, but in some countries it is a good answer to the problem. The best answer for all of us is, of course: use your fresh water carefully.

This factory in Kuwait makes fresh water from sea water.

6.1 Were you right?

1 Look back at Activity 5.4. Then circle the best words in these sentences.

a When water changes to ice, it gets *bigger / smaller*.

b Icebergs are *sometimes / always* white.

c The *Arctic / Antarctic* has 70% of the world's fresh water in its ice.

d When icebergs float in the sea, they slowly get *bigger / smaller*.

2 Look at this picture of the *Titanic*. Find two mistakes in it.

1 ....

2 ....

6.2 What more did you learn?

Write the right numbers under the pictures.

1 This way is very expensive and difficult. It works, but it takes a long time.

2 This way works well. It is expensive but many countries use it.

3 This way is very expensive and only works sometimes.

6.3 Language in use

Look at the sentences in the box. Put these words into the sentences below.

> We **can't** make more water.
>
> We **can**, perhaps, find new ground water.

can	can't	could	couldn't

1   We .... make a lake with a dam across a river.

2   The Egyptians .... use the Nile floods on their farms.

3   An aeroplane with chemicals .... make rain without clouds.

4   The *Titanic* .... stop and it hit the iceberg.

5   You .... make fresh water from sea water, but it is expensive.

6   We .... use sea water on our farms.

7   The water was dirty, so we .... drink it.

8   Where .... we see the world's biggest fresh water factory?

6.4 What's next?

The last chapter looks at our use of water. Discuss these sentences. What do you think? Are they right (✓) or wrong (✗)?

1   Farms use more water than factories.

2   Every European and North American uses more than 100 litres of water every day.

3   Farmers don't use ground water.

4   Factories use 450,000 litres of water for one car.

5   Factories pollute the air and the water near them.

6   There are 1,000,000,000 people in the world without clean water.

CHAPTER 6

What can we do?

We have to think about those people in the world without clean water – and about the future for our children's children.

We have to use our fresh water more carefully – all of us. But who uses most of the water?

Nearly three quarters of the people in the world have water only from rivers and wells. Many people in Africa and Asia have only 10 litres of water each day. Five thousand children die every day in the world because their water carries diseases.

In the United Kingdom, each person drinks and cooks with about three litres of water, but they also use 60 litres or more for baths and clean clothes. Fifty litres go down the toilet every day. Britons wash their cars and water their gardens, all with good, clean water. Each person uses more than 140 litres every day. Water use is about the same in other European countries.

Americans use more. Each man and woman in the United States uses about 200 litres every day, half of it in the bathroom. Rich people in California use more. A lot of them swim in fresh water in their gardens. But in the United States there are also about 4,000,000 people without clean water in their homes.

In Australia most people live in the big cities near the sea. They use 200 litres of water every day too. But there are droughts nearly every year. The farms have no water, and the problem is getting worse.

● The problem of farms

We use more water on farms and in factories than in our homes – a lot more. Every day there are about 220,000 more people on Earth, and they all need water. But they also need food, and this food comes from farms – from plants and from animals (for meat and milk). Without water, these plants and animals will die. Usually, most of this water comes from rain. But rainfall can, of course, be a big problem.

Too much rain causes floods; then plants and sometimes animals die. In a drought, the ground gets very dry. Then too, plants and animals sometimes die. Some countries have a lot of rain, but they use only about 10% of it. The other 90% goes back into the ground, the air or the sea. Other countries have very little rain, and farming is only possible near rivers.

Farmers use river water and ground water.

So all over the world, when the weather is dry, farmers take water from rivers and lakes. They water their fruit and vegetables and also give it to their animals. In most countries they also pump up a lot of ground water and put it on their land. In this way the plants stay green and the people in the cities get their food.

But what happens then to the rivers and the ground water? Some rivers are dry. In some places wells are dry too. One day, perhaps, there will be no ground water in some countries.

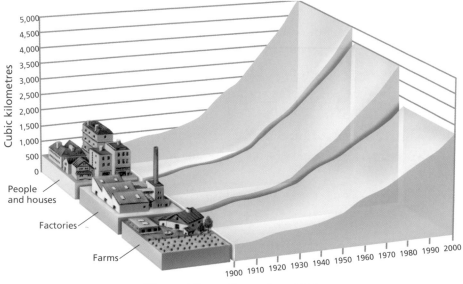

The world's use of water from 1900

● Dry rivers and lakes

In Asia, between Kazakhstan and Uzbekistan, there are two great rivers: the Amu Darya and the Syr Darya. In 1918, the Russians started to take water from them and make farmland. The farms were very big and a lot of food came from them. But the two rivers ran into the Aral Sea, a great lake. 35,000,000 people lived round the lake. 10,000 people caught fish in it. 3% of the fish in Russian shops came from the Aral Sea.

Forty years later, the Aral Sea was nearly dry. Most of the water from the rivers didn't arrive there. The Aral Sea is now a very small lake and the boats sit on dry land.

When the Aral Sea dried, people there had no work. Their boats were many kilometres from the water. The

The Aral Sea was dry.

36

water and the land were also very salty, and many people got ill. Today there is a new dam across one end of the Aral Sea. The lake is getting bigger, and there are fish in it again. But it is smaller than it was.

There are problems with river water everywhere. The Yellow River is more than 4,800 kilometres long and it runs across China. A lot of farmers take water from it. Cities and factories also take water from it. In 1972, the river didn't arrive at the sea. It was dry.

In California, in the United States, 25,000,000 people take water from the great Colorado River for their cities, factories and farms. Now very little water arrives in Mexico. The river is nearly dry.

● The problem of factories

Factories also cause problems. People need food and water, but they also need houses, clothes, cars, computers, paper and televisions. Factories make these, and factories use a lot of fresh water. They use 450,000 litres of water for a family car, and 400 litres for one kilo of paper. About 22% of the world's fresh water goes into factories. In the richer countries, it is more than half.

Factories can pollute the air and the water near them.

A lot of the water runs out of the factories again, into rivers and the sea. Often this water is then dangerously dirty. It can pollute river and sea water and kill the fish in hours.

Factories can also pollute the air with their smoke. Rain from this dirty air is not clean. In many countries factories have to clean their smoke before it goes into the air. But not in all countries, and not all factories.

Today, in most countries, factories also have to be careful with their water. They have to clean it before it goes into the ground or into a river. But mistakes and accidents happen all the time. We have to do better.

● Pollution everywhere

But in most countries the biggest problem with pollution is from farms. The farmers put a lot of chemicals on the land. These chemicals make the plants bigger and stronger, and people have more food. But the chemicals go down into the ground water. The rain also washes the chemicals into the rivers. They pollute the water and kill the fish. There are chemicals from farmland in 90% of the rivers in Europe.

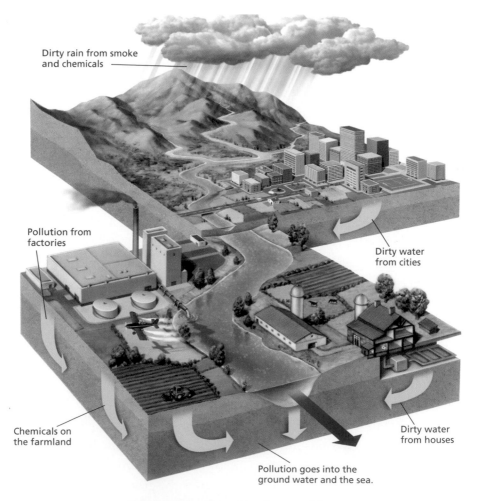

Dirty rain from smoke and chemicals

Pollution from factories

Dirty water from cities

Chemicals on the farmland

Dirty water from houses

Pollution goes into the ground water and the sea.

Pollution comes from cities, farms and factories.

So, that is one of the big problems. We need more water every year, for our cities, our farms and our factories. But those cities, farms and factories all make the water too dirty for our use.

Clean water for all

Everybody needs water. But some people have too much and most people have too little. We can make new lakes behind dams. We can pump up ground water and move it to our cities. We can take water from rivers and lakes for our farms. We can also get water from ice and sea water. It is difficult and expensive, but it is possible.

But people in rich countries have to think hard about their use of water. They have to stop polluting rivers, ground water and the seas. They have to use their clean water more carefully. And they have to help people without clean water in other countries.

What can *we* do? How can *we* help?

We can think about our use of water every day. We need to think when we cook. We need to think when we wash. We have to think about those people in the world without clean water – and about the future for our children's children.

World plans for the future

Every year, 22 March is World Water Day. This began in 1992 in Rio de Janeiro at a big meeting of the United Nations. That year, people from every country in the world met and discussed plans for the future. How could we make the world a better place? Every year on 22 March, each country makes new plans for cleaner water for more of their people.

They want to help the 1,000,000,000 people in the world without clean water – before it is too late.

1 Work with another student. Who has worse problems?

a Make notes before you talk about it.

Student A	In your country there are a lot of floods. They are getting worse every year. You think you have bigger problems than Student B. Why?

Student B	In your country there are a lot of droughts. They are getting worse every year. You think you have bigger problems than Student A. Why?

b Have the conversation in front of the class. What do they think? Who does have worse problems?

2 Work with other students. Discuss this question. Use the ideas below.

How can rich countries help countries with water problems?

Ideas

Money
(for food, houses, hospitals and schools ...)
But who gets the money?
What can people do with it?

People
(doctors, teachers, farmers ...)
But who pays these people?
Where do they live?
What can they do?

They can send:

Things
(pumps, food ...)
But how can they send them?
What will people do with them?

1 You are going to write about China's water problems for a magazine. Look at the photos. One is of a place in the Himalayas in 1968. The other is the same place now. How are they different?

2 Now read these notes.

China - BIG country
(1,400,000,000 people) - getting bigger

Nearly half of fresh water from
Himalayas (mountains)
Ice and snow melts in spring - water
runs into Yellow and Yangtze rivers
- for cities and farms

Winters warmer - 7% more ice melting
each year
In future (50 years?)
little ice and snow - problems

3 Write your story.

The Arctic is a very cold place, but people live there. Some of these people are Inuit. There are about 160,000 Inuit in Alaska, the north of Canada and Greenland.

Where the Inuits now live

Where the Inuits used to live

Russia

Arctic Ocean

Greenland

Alaska (United States)

North Atlantic Ocean

North Pacific Ocean

Canada

1 Work with three or four other students. Discuss these questions and find answers in books or on the Internet.

a What do Inuit live in, now and in the past? How did they build houses from ice? Draw one.

b What do Inuit eat? Where do they get their food? Draw one of their foods.

c What are the names of Inuit boats? Draw one.

2 **The Inuit people are having problems.**

   a Read this letter from an Inuit to a newspaper.

> To the people of the world!
>
> The Inuit people in the Arctic are having a lot of problems, and *you* are causing them. In Greenland and Canada, we live very near the sea ice. We catch our food on it. When I was a boy, the sea ice came every November. Today, it comes two or three months later. The weather is changing and the ice melts quickly. The sea is flooding the land. Some of our villages are now under the sea.
>
> We have to walk on the ice when we catch animals and fish for our food. But the ice is often thinner and weaker now and this is very dangerous. Some of our men fell through the ice into the water last year and died.
>
> Everything is changing. Why is this happening to us? It is because your cities, your cars, your aeroplanes and your factories are making the world's air warmer. You are changing the weather of our world. You are talking about your problems in fifty years. We are having the problems NOW. It has to stop. You have to do something before it is too late.
>
> *Paul Karetak*
>
> Paul Karetak
> Iqaluit, Nunavut, Canada

   b Have this conversation.

| **Student A** | You work for the newspaper. You want to write more in your paper about the Inuit and their life. Talk to the Inuit man and his family about his people and their problems. |
| **Students B–E** | You are the Inuit man and his family. Answer the questions. |

3 **John Day lived for three years with the Inuit people in Greenland. He also walked across the Arctic. He is a very interesting man and has an exciting life.**

He is living for a time in a town near you. You would like him to come to your school with pictures of the Inuit and his walks, and talk to everybody. Write a letter to him.

A LONG
COLD WALK
FOR JOHN

4 **John is going to come to your school. Make a poster (with pictures) about his visit. Put the place and the time on it, and something about John and his interesting life.**